ENGLISH SILVERSMITHS' WORK

A GOLDSMITHS' WORKSHOP in the reign of Charles II
from *A new Touch-Stone for Gold and Silver Wares* by William Badcock, London, 1679.

KEY

6 The Test Mould.

7 A Wind-hole to melt Silver in without Bellows.

8 A pair of Organ-Bellows.

9 A man melting or Boiling or (an)nealing Silver at them.

10 A Block with a large Anvil placed thereon.

11 Three Men Forging Plate.

12 The Fineing and other Goldsmiths' Tools.

13 The Assay furnace.

14 The Assay-Master making Assays.

15 His Man putting Assays into the Fire.

16 The Warden marking the Plate on the Anvil.

17 His Officer holding the Plate for the Marks.

VICTORIA AND ALBERT MUSEUM

English Silversmiths' Work

CIVIL AND DOMESTIC: AN INTRODUCTION

By Charles Oman

LONDON

HER MAJESTY'S STATIONERY OFFICE

1965

First published 1965

© Crown copyright 1965

Copies of this book may be had
from the Victoria and Albert Museum bookstall
and from H.M. Stationery Office
at the following addresses:
York House, Kingsway, London W.C.2
423 Oxford Street, London W.1
13A Castle Street, Edinburgh 2
109 St. Mary Street, Cardiff
39 King Street, Manchester 2
50 Fairfax Street, Bristol 1
35 Smallbrook, Ringway, Birmingham 5
80 Chichester Street, Belfast 1
or through any bookseller.

Obtainable in the United States of America
from the British Information Services,
845 Third Avenue, New York 22, N.Y.

Price £2 2s. 0d.

*Printed in England for Her Majesty's Stationery Office
by The Curwen Press, London*

FOREWORD

Over forty years have elapsed since the appearance of the CATALOGUE OF ENGLISH SILVER, CIVIL AND DOMESTIC compiled by the late W. W. Watts, then Keeper of the Department of Metalwork. That work was so successful in drawing the attention of the public to the collection and attracting benefactions, that it became obsolete long before the stock of copies was exhausted. The present volume has been compiled by Mr Charles Oman, Keeper of the Department of Metalwork, and is intended to provide an introduction to the collection as it was at the close of 1961.

TRENCHARD COX
Director

LATE MEDIEVAL SILVER

(1375-1525)

THE amount of plate in secular use in England during the Middle Ages was always limited, although it was certainly increasing towards the close. Quite a lot was in use in the monastic refectories and most of this got melted down at the time of their spoliation by Henry VIII. About the same time lay owners were treating their plate in the same manner, since it had become unfashionable after the arrival of the Renaissance style.

Leaving out of consideration spoons, which will form the subject of a separate monograph, the surviving examples of medieval domestic plate are mostly either drinking vessels or salts (the museum has no example of the latter).

The earliest piece is the Studley Bowl (pls. 1 and 2) which owes its name to the fact that it was for a time the property of Studley Royal Church near Ripon. It is engraved with a black letter alphabet and with contractions, and was perhaps intended to aid the education of some child of wealthy parents.

The most popular form of drinking vessel, used specially by the middle class and the lower clergy, was the mazer. It was of turned maple wood and, since silver was only needed for the lip-band and for the enamelled boss or 'print' in the centre, it was relatively inexpensive and hardly worth scrapping after it had gone out of fashion. The Rokewode Mazer (pl. 3), which owes its name to a recent owner, has its lip-band engraved with a verse which, when modernized, reads: 'Hold your tongue and say the best, And let your neighbours sit in rest, Whoso listeth God to please, Let his neighbour live in ease.' The Cromwell Mazer (pl. 4) illustrates the characteristic form in use in the 15th century, which had a shallower bowl but a deeper lip-band. It was formerly the property of the Lambert family, who had received it as a gift from Richard Cromwell sometime Lord Protector.

In Anglo-Saxon days drinking-horns were in general use, but by the later Middle Ages they retained only the prestige of being connected with the good old days. According to tradition the Pusey Horn (pl. 5) was given together with the manor of Pusey, Berks, by Cnut to one of his officers who had penetrated in disguise into the Saxon camp and returned with news of an impending attack. In time the horn became a classic example of the feudal tenure of 'Cornage', a variety of 'Grand Serjeanty' and was produced in court in 1684 before Lord Chancellor Jeffries in the course of a lawsuit. As a work of art the horn dates only from the first half of the 15th century when it was mounted up in silver-gilt. The band to which the legs are attached, is inscribed in black letters: 'I Kyng Knowde geve Wyllyam Pecote thys horne to holde by thy londe.' It would appear that the silversmith made a double misreading of the inscription given to him for copying. Thus he read the 'w' of 'Pewse' as 'co' and the long 's' as 't'. The horn remained associated with the manor of Pusey until the final abolition of feudal tenures by Lord Birkenhead's Law of Property Act of 1922.

The Kimpton Bowl is an attractive example of the small type of art in use towards the end of the 15th century. It served as a chalice at Kimpton church, Hants, until it was acquired by the museum.

England was one of the earliest countries to introduce the practice of hall-marking. A statute of 1300 authorized the wardens of the London goldsmiths to mark with a leopard's head all new plate but although the system of marking was elaborated in the course of the 14th and 15th centuries, it will be found that none of the pieces mentioned heretofore are marked at all. Towards the end of the 15th century the Goldsmiths' Company began to make a greater effort to enforce the law and introduced marking with an annual letter which enables pieces to be dated exactly. A great many pieces of 16th and 17th century date are found with the goldsmith's mark only, this being all that was legally necessary (before 1697) for pieces made for private order. Completely unmarked pieces obviously of London manufacture, like the handsome serpentine bowl mounted in silver-gilt (pl. 7a), become rarer but some flagrantly illegal pieces were made. Thus the 'Ordinances of the Goldsmiths' of 1370, forbade the making of cups, etc. of copper or latten-gilt but the example illustrated (pl. 8b) which is complete with a scriptural text enjoining sobriety, must have been made about the same time as the Campion Cup (pl. 8a) which has the 1500–1 hall-mark.

RENAISSANCE SILVER

(1525–1625)

THE Renaissance began to affect English plate in the third decade of the 16th century. The Howard Grace Cup (pls. 9 and 10) is typical of the brief phase during which Gothic and Renaissance ornament appear together on the same piece. Soon all traces of medieval ornament disappear, but the rapid spreading of the use of Renaissance detail did not affect the shapes of many types of plate which continued to develop gradually throughout the century.

The introduction of the Renaissance style to England must be ascribed partly to the presence of foreign artists like Hans Holbein (who designed plate for Henry VIII), but a more potent influence was the continuous importation of the printed designs issued by the silversmiths of Germany and the Low Countries. These imported designs were more often imitated than copied, and the English silversmith frequently combined on one piece motifs borrowed from the engravings by different foreign artists. The marine subjects on the set of dishes of 1573, formerly belonging to the Montagu Family (pls. 17 to 20) are imitated from the work of the Antwerp artist, Adriaen Collaert, and are in nowise related to the scenes from the stories of Abraham and of Isaac which they surround.

Much Tudor plate went to the melting-pot during the Civil War, and it will be noted that a large proportion of the pieces illustrated are not made of silver throughout, but are only silver mounted; and these doubtless owe their survival to the smallness of their silver content, which made them hardly worth melting.

The objects mounted in silver were sometimes selected because of great rarity or beauty, such as the agate cup (pl. 16), the jug of Turkish earthenware (pl. 21), and the Chinese porcelain wine-jug (pl. 22). It is less easy to account for the large number of Rhenish brown earthenware jugs which were mounted up in silver during the second half of the 16th century (pls. 15 and 24). These were certainly never rare, and appear nowadays much less attractive than the silver-mounted mazers which by the reign of Elizabeth were fast falling into disfavour. Coconut cups (pl. 25), however, remained fairly popular.

The collection does not include any large Elizabethan silver cup. The covered cup of 1590 (pl. 29) is important as an illustration of the beginning of a return to simple forms, which was destined to become more marked during the next reign. The Smelt Cup (pl. 32), which is here shown without its Jacobean cover, is more typical of the medium-sized drinking vessel in use at the close of the period.

The collection is fortunate in possessing examples of three of the more popular forms of large Elizabethan salt (pls. 27 and 30), as well as several small salts (pls. 12 and 31). The cylindrical salt which once formed part of the plate of Mostyn Hall is particularly notable for its finely embossed arabesques. The sides of the square Vyvyan Salt are filled with paintings under glass, adapted from Geoffrey Whitney's *Emblems and Other Devices*, etc., published at Leyden in 1586. Bell-shaped salts made their appearance in the middle of the 16th century, and form a link between the great salt and the small one. In reality they consist of two salts, fitting one above the other and surmounted by a cover with a perforated knob to serve as a caster.

Before the use of forks became general, a ewer and basin formed a very necessary part of the equipment of the dining hall. This collection includes a fine ewer
of 1583 (pl. 26), and a basin of 1607 (pl. 36).

Amongst the smaller pieces should be noted the snuffers (pl. 11), which bear
an inscription indicating that they formed part of the furnishing of the Privy
Council Chamber in the reign of Edward VI.

During this period important pieces of plate were generally gilt. Only two
of the pieces illustrated (pls. 23 and 25) are of plain silver.

EARLY STUART SILVER

(1625–50)

THE plate of the Early Stuart Period was marked by continuous change both
in the form and the decoration, therein contrasting strongly with the almost static
Elizabethan and Charles II work.

The influence of the sheets of engraved ornament issued by German silversmiths is still apparent in the reign of James I and can be traced in the bands of
embossed fruit and cartouches on the tankard of 1607 (pl. 35) and still more in the
engraved hunting scenes on the standing cup of 1611 (pls. 37 and 38) which was
made by a silversmith from whose hand a little group of masterpieces remain but
whose name is unknown.

A wide range of small drinking cups was made about the same time having
slender baluster stems and bowls of various patterns (pl. 39 and 40). The bowls
of the large cups were usually egg-shaped and the most popular form of finial for
the cover took the form of a 'pyramid' (nowadays called a steeple). 'Pyramids'
were used to surmount both cups (pls. 41, 45 and 46) and, more rarely, salts (pl. 42).
This was the last variety of the great salt in the full medieval tradition and was
followed in the reign of Charles I by a much more modest variety with a low
spool-shaped body which appears to have been introduced from the Continent.

During the Middle Ages and Renaissance, plate of any importance was gilt.
From the middle of the reign of James I it became increasingly usual to leave it
plain. This was accompanied by an increasing use of simple forms and decoration
(pl. 47). This tendancy became accentuated in the reign of Charles I (pls. 48, 49 and
52) but it should also be remembered that much of the more ornate plate perished
early to fill the coffers of King or Parliament during the Civil War. Besides the

plate without applied decoration, there was a considerable output of silver engraved in a broad manner (pl. 50) or decorated with punched ornament (pl. 51).

The outbreak of the Civil War affected English silver in several ways. The
small but not unimportant number of foreign silversmiths returned home, so that
imported sheets of engraved ornament (by now mainly Dutch), became the sole
external influence on English silversmiths. This, however, did not make much
difference as not only was an immense amount of plate melted down, but the
general distress and uncertainty reduced the demand for new plate.

Of course there were still fine craftsmen to execute important orders when they
did appear. The richly decorated flagon (pl. 54) bears the mark *a hound sejant*
of a silversmith whose name has not been discovered but whose clients are
mostly known to have been Royalists. It seems likely that this piece which bears the
hall-mark for 1646 and the arms of a Dutch merchant resident in London, must
have a connection with some Royalist intrigue.

CHARLES II PERIOD

(1651–1688)

DURING the ten years of King Charles's exile the silversmiths had been working
short hours but trade had not been entirely stagnant. Much of the work done
during the Commonwealth reflects in its simplicity the financial stringency of the
times. A certain amount of work had come along from those who had done well
out of the Civil War and the Commonwealth, and also from those whose family
circumstances had allowed them to remain aloof from politics. Customers who
were able to afford more elaborate workmanship could, however, still find highly
skilled craftsmen. The tankard (pls. 57 and 58) made in 1657 by John Plummer of
York copies a popular Danish pattern which was fitted inside with pegs to serve in
drinking bouts. It is one of a small group very finely engraved with flowers
inspired (but not copied) by the contemporary herbals.

The Charles II style was already fully formed when in 1660 silversmithing was
resumed on a large scale as a result of the increasing commercial prosperity and
return of public confidence which followed upon the Restoration. Hardly any of the
pieces here illustrated show any overlap of the forms or of the decoration of the
earlier part of the century. The most notable exception is the Moody Salt (pl. 63)
which belongs to the latest variety of the great salt which by now was becoming

obsolete owing to the abandonment of the old traditional ritual of the dining hall. The disappearance of this last custom did not signify any return to simpler habits, as fashion was ever finding fresh ways of using silver. Though the collection is made up mainly of pieces of a more or less utilitarian nature, the ostentatious use of silver is illustrated by the handsome garniture of a vase and pair of flasks from the Ashburnham Collection (pls. 69 and 70), the rich, but by no means unique toilet service once belonging to the old Yorkshire family of Calverley (pls. 79–81). and one of the earliest known wine-coolers which weighs 232 oz. 18 dwt. (pl. 71). Silver hearth equipment will be found at Ham House. English silversmiths, however, had kept themselves abreast of continental developments by studying imported engravings of designs, so that though in 1660 the personnel of the silversmithing industry was almost entirely English, its outlook was by no means insular. Within a short time of the Restoration a sprinkling of foreign silversmiths came to share in the returning prosperity, but there can be little doubt that imported engravings remained the main medium of foreign influence. It is, however, extremely difficult to separate the two strains since the more prosperous foreigners (German, Swiss, Dutch, French and Flemings) sometimes employed English goldsmiths with registered marks, whilst the less successful foreigners were employed in English workshops.

In the ensuing quarter of a century English silver shows extraordinarily little sign of development either in form or decoration. The forms of the various types of drinking vessels appear to have been developed mainly in this country, though contacts with Scandinavia affected the shape of some of the tankards made in North East England (pl. 67). It is less easy to decide on the derivation of the forms of the vessels required for the consumption of tea, coffee and chocolate which were becoming increasingly fashionable. The earliest silver tea-pot (pl. 66) is only known as such because of the inscription which records its presentation to the Committee of the East India Company to whom the simple but rather better proportioned coffee-pot (pl. 74) also formerly belonged. The later tea-pot (pl. 89) owes its much more attractive form to a variety of Chinese earthenware wine-pots. An ornamental vase (pl. 7) provides another instance of the use of a Chinese form. Dutch and French sources can be recognized for the forms of many of the other pieces.

Whilst there can be no doubt that Dutch fashions formed the predominant influence on English plate at this period, they did not enjoy a monopoly nor were they undiluted. The collection possesses as yet no good example of the fish forms popularized by the engravings of the great Dutch silversmith Christian van Vianen. The popular motif of *putti* amongst acanthus leaves which appears on the Calverley

Toilet Service (pl. 79b) seems to have been derived from the engraved designs of Jean le Pautre and Polifilo Zancarli and was widely used both in France and Holland. Chinese and Indian motifs decorate much Charles II plate, but only occasionally is it possible to recognize any real appreciation of oriental art as on the little box traditionally connected with Nell Gwynn (pl. 90). For the most part, fantastic Chinese figures and exotic birds and flowers provided all the oriental flavour that was required (pls. 75, 76 and 87). The collection is rich in examples of heraldic engravings showing the varieties of squarish shield fashionable at this time and usually accompanied by a decoration of plumes or of palm-branches. The custom of showing the heraldic tinctures by different forms of hatching was still unusual. The most interesting association disclosed by the heraldic achievement is that of the cup of 1683 (pl. 80) which bears the arms of Thomas Pengelly impaling those of his wife Rachel Baines. In the year in which this cup was made its owners invited the ex-Lord Protector Richard Cromwell to come to live with them, an arrangement which lasted until their death.

QUEEN ANNE DOMESTIC SILVER

(1689–1727)

THE Queen Anne Period includes in fact the reigns of both of the queen's predecessors and successor. Dutch influence which had been of great importance during the reign of Charles II declined after the Revolution and was replaced by French. William III undoubtedly liked French art but of much greater importance was the fact that he reigned in England as the Protestant champion. In 1685 Louis XIV had revoked the Edict of Nantes leaving the Huguenot silversmiths the alternative of conforming or emigrating. A considerable number of Huguenot silversmiths, mainly from the larger provincial towns of northern and western France, arrived in England where a government wedded to the cause of Protestantism was bound to protect them. It was not long before the English silversmiths discovered that the Huguenots were serious rivals and were seeking to have their activities restricted. A very frank petition in 1711 to the Worshipful Company of Goldsmiths signed by some quite well-known London silversmiths states 'That by the admission of necessitous strangers whose desperate fortunes obliged them to work at miserable rates, the representing members have been forced to bestow much more time and labour in working up their plate than hath been the practice in former times, when prices of workmanship were much greater'.

Though the government felt bound to hold the balance between the English and Huguenot silversmiths, they regarded their joint activities as highly detrimental to the national economy. A shortage of silver for currency was attributed to an excessive use of the metal for the manufacture of plate. In order to discourage the latter use an act of Parliament was passed making compulsory a higher standard containing 11 oz. 10 dwt. of pure silver in each pound (troy) instead of 11 oz. 2 dwt. as heretofore. The New Sterling or Britannia Standard (as it was called from one of the new marks), came into force on 27th March, 1697 and remained compulsory until 31st May, 1720, when its use was made optional. As an attempt to discourage the manufacture of plate by raising the cost, it would seem to have been a complete failure, as the purchasing public was prepared to face the extra expense.

Considering that the aim of the government was to discourage the extravagant use of plate, it treated the Huguenot silversmiths with remarkable indulgence. English silversmiths at the close of the 17th century still preferred to use fairly thin silver which they could decorate with embossing and engraving. The Huguenots, on the other hand, tended to follow the French tradition of workmanship, making much use of cast work which involved a much greater expenditure of metal. The lighter English tradition persisted with ever diminishing popularity right into the reign of George I and is characterized by the frequent use of fluting and gadrooning, combined with roped borders. Engraved and embossed chinoiserie, so extensively used in the latter years of Charles II, went out of favour earlier. The Huguenot silversmiths who reached England, had not generally been of much note in their own country but had been trained in an exacting school and circumstances had sharpened their wits. They had a flair for good shapes and for the skilful use of simple mouldings and faceting, enhanced by cast and applied details as well as 'cut-card work' (designs cut in thin sheet metal and soldered on the body of a piece). Their efforts soon won the approval of the wealthier customers and at an early date English silversmiths learnt to imitate them, so that ultimately the two styles merged.

The collection still lacks examples of some of the most characteristic plate of the period, such as the monumental wine-cisterns, punch-bowls and 'monteiths' (a variety of punch-bowl fitted with a detachable scalloped rim which allowed it to be used for a wine-glass cooler). The smaller varieties are well represented and illustrated, within their limits, the forms and decoration of this period. It should be remembered that there was already considerable specialization within the silversmith's craft, so that the master whose mark appears on a piece cannot be presumed to have conceived it entirely himself, far less executed it. One of the most distinct associated crafts was that of the engravers. The illustrations bear witness to their superb craftsmanship but it was contrary to trade practice for them to sign their work (as they did when working for the printers). An exception, however, was Joseph Sympson who signed several salvers which he engraved (pl. 109) and who won a grudging reference in Horace Walpole's *Catalogue of Engravers*.

This section is not rich in historical associations but the flask (pl. 107) passed on the death of General Charles Churchill to his brother the first Duke of Marlborough, who also had his arms engraved upon it. The little taperstick (pl. 102) was formerly the property of Charles Kingsley who inherited it as a family heirloom with the tradition that it had been given by Queen Anne to an ancestress, Mrs. Kingsley, who had been governess to the Queen's son the Duke of Gloucester.

MID-GEORGIAN SILVER

(1728-1770)

THE Mid-Georgian period comprehends the interval between the fading out of the 'Queen Anne' style in the latter years of George I and the arrival of the 'Adam' style ten years after George III had come to the throne.

The taste for very large pieces of silver was in abeyance and silversmiths who ventured to make such as a speculation, were apt to find them difficult to sell. Porcelain, both Oriental and European, was beginning to compete seriously in the market for lesser domestic pieces. None the less, the middle of the 18th century saw the manufacture of a very large quantity of medium and small plate. It was a period characterized by the lavish use of ornament, though it should be remembered that relatively plain pieces were also produced for those with simple tastes or limited means. In the latter part of the reign of George I the rich and regularly arranged 'Louis XIV' ornament had come into favour and its use continued into the early years of his successor (pls. 115 and 118). A more obvious break with the 'Queen Anne' tradition is shown by the decoration of classical gods and goddesses on the tea-kettle made in about the same year by C. Kandler (pl. 117), which is probably based on some German design. The movement away from the tradition of simple forms and plain mouldings is visible in greater or less extent in all the early pieces here shown.

The Rococo style was evolved in Paris mainly by Juste-Aurèle Meissonnier, an architect, who was admitted to the Paris gild of goldsmiths in 1725. It was characterized by the combination of richness with irregularity and its ornament broken scrolls and shells were favourite motifs. Some English silversmiths, like Paul de Lamerie, were more susceptible than others to this new wave of French influence but by 1740 it was in general demand, though some conservative clients seem to have insisted on the continuation of the older fashion. The repertoire of ornament used by the Mid-Georgian silversmiths was not limited to variations of the two motifs already mentioned. Some of them went quite far afield in search of inspiration but the two most important sources are naturalistic floral designs and chinoiserie. Both were used independently but are generally found combined with Rococo motifs.

In the earlier part of the present period ' Queen Anne' shapes continued in use more or less disguised by the new types of applied ornament. Gradually, as the Rococo style became predominant, fresh forms were evolved. Pear-shaped and inverted pear-shaped bodies were much favoured.

A curious example of the reproduction in silver of a contemporary Staffordshire ware design, is afforded by a tea-pot (pl. 135) made in 1748 by John Wirgman. In general, however, the interrelation of the silversmith's and the potter's arts was the other way round. A design for a silver soup-tureen serves as a reminder that Nicholas Sprimont designed silver as well as Chelsea porcelain (pl. 141).

In contrast to the previous period extensive use was made of embossed decoration. Another technique which was more fully exploited was that of piercing, which was found especially suitable for the ornamentation of cake-baskets (pl. 138) and sweetmeat dishes. The most effective instance of this technique, however, was made in the decoration of the 'cheese plate' (as it was described in the original bill), formerly at Burghley House (pl. 142). The high standard of chasing was maintained whilst the scope of the engravers was not so rigidly confined to heraldic adornment. Unfortunately, no piece in the collection bears the engraver's signature. The quality of the heraldic engraving continued high. The grand manner is illustrated by the rendering of the arms (pl. 115) on the salver made by John Hugh Le Sage for the famous Earl of Chesterfield who in 1727 was just beginning his political career. The engravers employed by Paul de Lamerie were highly skilled, and there is good reason for believing that the Walpole Salver (pl. 118) was engraved for him by William Hogarth. This piece had been made out of the silver of the Exchequer Seal which became the perquisite of the Chancellor whenever it became necessary to order a new one. Sir Robert Walpole was able to collect two salvers during his long term of this office. The principal motif of the central roundel is copied from the back and front of the seal, the rest of space being occupied by a view of London and allegorical figures. Thomas Farren's engravers remain anonymous but have left many memorials of their capacity; a good example of their work is on the salver (pls. 125–6) made in 1733 for John Shales Barrington who was very proud of his mother's royal descent. Its perfect condition is owed in part to the fact that it was probably never used during the lifetime of its first owner. About the time that the salver must have been delivered to him, he was crossed in love and thereafter he lived as a recluse at his house at Waltham Cross. It is still in pristine condition.

ADAM SILVER

(1771–1800)

THE changeover from the Rococo to the Adam style in about 1770, was rapid and as complete as any of the alterations of taste which have affected English silver. Robert Adam returned from Italy in 1758, steeped in the beauties of classical art which was receiving much publicity owing to the successful excavations at Herculaneum (begun 1738) and Pompeii (begun 1755). He did not have to wait long for popularity and by the time that the Greco-Roman style began to be reflected in the form and decoration of English silver, he had been for some years the most fashionable architect in the country. He was not content with providing houses for his clients but was very ready to design the fittings and accessories as well. A number of his designs for plate and a quantity of plate from his designs have survived but, unfortunately, none are in this Museum; some of his designs are to be found in the library of Sir John Soane's Museum.

It should be emphasized that though Adam silver is heavily indebted to Greco-Roman art, it owes little to Greco-Roman plate. Little of the last was available at the period, so that would-be designers were obliged to seek inspiration from pieces in other materials, generally marble. Some classical forms lent themselves easily to adaptation for modern needs. Covered cups (pls. 150, 155 and 181), tea-caddies (pls. 164 and 173) and tureens (pls. 160 and 176) could be copied without difficulty from the large range of classical urns. More ingenuity, however, was required in the designing of candlesticks (pls. 156 and 157), coffee-pots (pl. 162), hot-water jugs (pl. 161), tea-pots (pl. 171) and wine-coolers (pl. 158).

The pieces just quoted represent serious attempts by their designers to produce results which were as nearly correct archaeologically as was reasonable. Much

Adam plate makes no attempt at correctness but is no more than vaguely classical in form, or decorated with plausible renderings of classical motifs. Although the purists of the Regency period deplored such pieces, time has not endorsed their criticisms, but has tended to accept the pleasing results without bothering about archaeological correctness.

The Adam style was the English manifestation of the wave of classical imitation which swept over Europe in the last quarter of the 18th century. The more serious English adaptations of classical designs exerted little influence abroad. Those foreign customers who could afford the more elaborate detail and careful finish, generally preferred to get their plate from Paris. The less serious Adam silver, evolved to suit the taste and the purses of the English middle class, was extensively imitated abroad, particularly in Scandinavia and in Portugal, by silver-smiths who worked for the same sort of clientèle. It also suited the taste and the pockets of the newly liberated American colonists.

It is not necessary to detail the classical motifs borrowed by the Adam silver-smiths but attention must be drawn to several characteristic techniques. The most obvious is the 'bright-cut' engraving used either to relieve plain surfaces (pls. 169, 177 and 178) or to enrich pierced ornament which had remained very popular (pls. 165 and 175). Fluting was most skilfully used (pls. 168, 173, 178 and 179). Little stamped medallions, founded upon James Tassie's reproductions of classical gems, were manufactured wholesale and used for the decoration of different types of plate (pls. 167 and 176). Little importance was attached to heraldic engraving which was sparingly used and generally of poor quality.

Classical art was not the only source of inspiration during this period. Rococo influence disappeared early, but sugar-bowls, etc., pierced with 'Chippendale Gothic' tracery are not uncommon (pl. 152). Chinoiserie motifs are also occasionally encountered (pl. 154) on objects on which their presence is appropriate.

Hitherto the London market had been supplied almost entirely by silver made in London. A significant development of this period is the entry of provincial silver-smiths into the London market. Ever since the beginning of the century the metal trades had been expanding in Birmingham and Sheffield. Latterly silversmithing had been developed and since the manufacturers resented having to send their wares long distances to be hall-marked, assay offices were established in both towns in 1773. Though the Birmingham silversmiths mostly made small wares of slight importance, the firm of Matthew Boulton and John Fothergill produced superb work (pl. 160). The Sheffield silversmiths were particularly noted for their candlesticks (pls. 156 and 157).

Meanwhile the old-established provincial silversmithing centres were faring variously. The silversmiths of Newcastle on Tyne were able to meet most of the requirements of the adjoining countryside, with well-made pieces of not very modern design. The assay office at York reopened in 1776 as the result of the establishment of the enterprising firms of Hampston & Prince which produced quite good work for the local market (pls. 169 and 170). The silversmiths of Chester and Exeter manufactured little but table silver.

REGENCY DOMESTIC SILVER

(1800-30)

ALTHOUGH the Regency actually lasted only from 4 February 1811 until 29 January 1820, during the whole of this period the development of English art owed much to the personal taste and patronage of the eldest son of George III. The Royal Collection at Windsor retains many traces of his patronage of the goldsmiths (as well as of his interest in antique plate), but a large number of the pieces here illustrated were made by the firms which worked for him, so that his influence seems to pervade the whole period.

By 1800 the Adam Style had lost its original vigour and those who sought to guide taste were looking out for fresh sources of inspiration. In 1806 Charles Heathcote Tatham, an architect, published a volume of Design for Ornamental Plate in the introduction to which he bewails the current fashions since 'instead of Massiveness, the principal characteristic of good Plate, light and insignificant forms have prevailed, to the utter exclusion of all good Ornament whatever'. Plate designed by Tatham certainly was massive and was derived from Roman Imperial Art which had now superseded the Greco-Roman fashion dominant during the Adam period. The same style was followed by all the identified designers of plate whose work is here illustrated – John Flaxman, R.A., Charles Catton junior, Thomas Stothard, R.A. and Benedetto Pistrucci.

Stothard's design for the Wellington Shield (pl. 205) is an example of classical art in modern dress, a change in taste which was already in evidence when the Deccan Plate was made in 1806 (pls. 189 and 190). The Renaissance traditions of representing contemporaries attired as Ancient Romans was now broken.

Unfortunately the collection is still without examples in fact derived from the use of Egyptian motifs in Roman imperial art. These became topical from the discoveries of the French archaeologists who had been taken to Egypt by

Napoleon, whose collected material fell into British hands after the Battle of Alexandria.

If Regency Art is mainly Neo-Classical, many other sources of inspiration are evident. The cult of antique plate had begun, and many pieces are imitations or adaptations of the work of earlier periods. Pieces in the Rococo style were extremely popular. Of the examples illustrated four (pls. 199b, 200 and 203) are pure Rococo, whilst a fifth (pl. 208) shows Rococo chinoiserie. Another piece (pl. 204) clearly foreshadows the Romantic style which was to become important in the reigns of William IV and Victoria.

All Regency plate does not show such eclecticism. Some of the less elaborate pieces merely continue the Adam style (pls. 183, 188a, 188b and 189) but others, such as the Newcastle salver engraved by Thomas Bewick (pl. 193) display a simplicity characteristic of the period.

Turning from the plate to its makers, it should be noted that the designers were frequently artists who had trained in other fields – architects, painters and sculptors. The genesis of many pieces is further complicated by the practice, already well-established, for a fashionable firm to hand out its commissions to be executed by others. Thus it will be found that of the many pieces inscribed RUNDELL, BRIDGE ET RUNDELL AURIFICES REGIS ET PRINCIPIS WALLIAE bear the maker's mark of Paul Storr or of Digby Scott and Benjamin Smith. It must not be supposed from this fact that the contribution of the firm of Royal Goldsmiths was entirely negligible for the second partner, John Bridge, was tireless in searching out talent. When obliged to set up its own workshop after parting association with Storr, the quality of its work showed no decline (pl. 207). The firm of Rundell, Bridge and Rundell, in point, dominated this period more completely than that of Paul de Lamerie had done up to the middle of the 18th century. Arbiters of taste like Tatham, laid much emphasis on the desirability of a high standard for chasing and there can be no doubt that quality of finish of the average piece of Regency silver will bear comparison with that of any of the preceding ones.

This section is particularly rich in pieces with historical associations. The fashion for presenting monumental pieces of plate to national heroes was now widespread. Lloyd's Patriotic Fund made extensive presentations on the occasion of Trafalgar. The admirals and some of the captains of ships present at the battle received vases valued at £300. The example illustrated (pl. 186) does not appear to have been awarded. No British general can ever have received so much presentation plate as the Duke of Wellington. The captions indicate the occasion for each presentation and only a few special comments are necessary. From the strictly historical point of view the most important pieces are the two (pls. 196 and 197) given by the officers of the British force which landed in Portugal in 1808. At the time that the subscriptions were collected, Sir Arthur Wellesley's conduct was the subject of a Court of Inquiry. The fact that his subordinates had raised a large sum for a presentation, was intended to indicate that they did not hold him responsible for the delay in following up his victories, nor for the terms of the Convention of Cintra, to which his signature was appended underneath those of his seniors, Sir Hew Dalrymple and Sir Harry Burrard. It is often forgotten that the Duke of Wellington was appointed ambassador to the Court of Louis XVIII on the overthrow of Napoleon in 1814. Since the 16th century it had been customary for newly appointed ambassadors to draw, from the Jewel Office, an allowance of plate so that they could keep up sufficient state whilst representing their sovereign abroad. After the Revolution of 1688, ambassadors (and the other officers who received this privilege), did not return their issues of plate on the completion of their term of office and in the course of time it came to be regarded as a perquisite. In the cleaning up of abuses after the Napoleonic Wars an end was made to this practice and the Duke's issue must have been nearly the last to be retained. It will be noted that the ambassadorial plate (pls. 195 and 199a) was not a specially designed service like the Deccan, but was assembled from what the shops had in stock.

NOTE

THE presentation to the Nation of Apsley House and its contents has greatly strengthened the collection of Regency plate belonging to the Victoria and Albert Museum. The captions recording a connection with the Duke of Wellington will naturally suggest to the reader that such pieces are to be seen at Apsley House, but the letter W.M. preceding the museum number will confirm that they do indeed belong to the Wellington Museum.

All other pieces are exhibited in the Victoria and Albert Museum.

1. THE STUDLEY BOWL. Silver-gilt. Late 14th century. H.5½ in.   M.1–1914

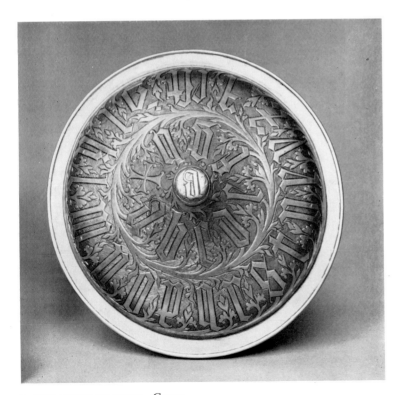

2. THE STUDLEY BOWL. Cover.

3a. THE ROKEWODE MAZER. Maple-wood mounted in silver-gilt. Late 14th century. Diam. 6⅓ in.
M.165–1914

3b. Inside view.

4a. THE CROMWELL MAZER. Maple-wood mounted in silver-gilt. Second half of 15th century. Purchased under the Francis Reubell Bryan Bequest. Diam. 8⅛ in.   M.129-1914

4b. Inside view.

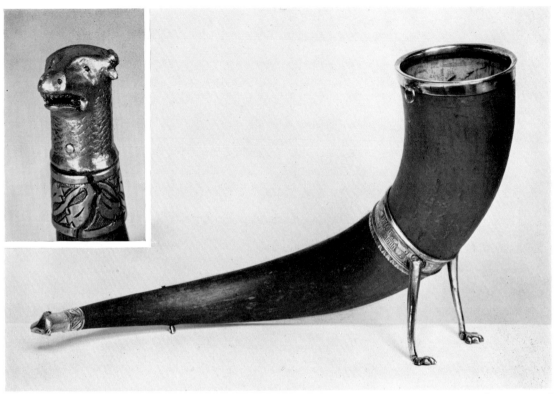

5a. THE PUSEY HORN. Horn mounted in silver-gilt. Early 15th century. Given by Mrs. Bouverie-Pusey, widow of Philip Bouverie-Pusey, of Pusey, Berks. H. 10 in.

5b. THE PUSEY HORN. Detail of tip (inset).   M.220–1938

6. THE KIMPTON BOWL. Silver-gilt. About 1480. H. 4⅛ in.   M.8–1931

7a. BOWL. Serpentine marble mounted in silver-gilt. Early 16th century. H. $3\frac{7}{8}$ in.   M.248–1924

7b. THE CHALKER MAZER. About 1490. D. $7\frac{3}{4}$ in.   45–1874

8a. THE CAMPION CUP. Maker's mark, a covered cup. London hall-mark for 1500–1. H. 3⅜ in.
M.249-1924

8b. CUP. Latten with traces of gilding outside and of tinning and gilding inside. About 1500. Croft Lyons Bequest. H. 5½ in.   M.880–1926

9. THE HOWARD GRACE CUP. Ivory mounted in silver-gilt set with pearls and garnets. Maker's mark, crossed implements. London hall-mark for 1525–26. H. 12 in. Given by Lord Wakefield through the National Art Collections Fund.   M.2680–1931

10a. THE HOWARD GRACE CUP. St. George.
M.2680–1931

10b. Details of cover and lip-band (VINVM. TVVM. BIBE. CVM. GAVDIO).

11. SNUFFERS from the Privy Council Chamber of Edward VI. 1547–53. L. 8 in. Acquired under the Bryan Bequest.

M.837–1928

12c. CASTER. Maker's mark illegible.
London hall-mark for 1563–64. H. 4⅛ in.
150–1886

12b. SALT. Maker's mark, crescent and three stars.
London hall-mark for 1563–64. H. 6 in.
147–1886

12a. SALT. Maker's mark, TA with a porcupine.
London hall-mark for 1566–67 (body);
1571–72 (cover). H. 5⅝ in.
148–1886

13a. JUG. Brown glazed earthenware mounted in silver-gilt. No marks. Middle of 16th century. H. 6 in.
M.351–1910

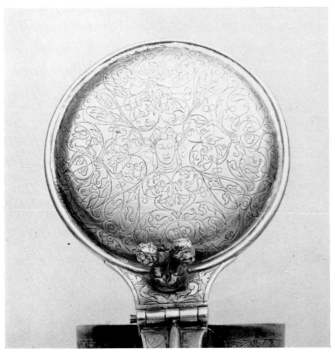

13b. Lid of M.351–1910.

14a. STANDING DISH. Maker's mark, A with a pellet. London hall-mark for 1564–65. H. 5⅞ in.

M.352–1912

14b. Inside view.

15. JUG. Rhenish stoneware mounted in silver-gilt. About 1560. H. $6\frac{1}{8}$ in.   2119–1855

16. CUP. Oriental agate mounted in silver-gilt. Maker's mark, ER in monogram. London hall-mark for 1567–68. H. 7⅞ in.   38–1867

17. PLATE (one of a set of six). Sacrifice of Issac. Maker's mark, FR conjoined. London hall-mark for 1573–74. D. 10 in. Acquired under the Murray Bequest with aid from the National Art Collections Fund.   M.55b–1946

18. PLATE (from the same set). Meeting of Rebecca and Isaac.   M.55d–1946

19. DETAIL of another plate from the same set.   M.55–1946

20. DETAIL of another plate from the same set.   M.55a–1946

21. JUG. Turkish earthenware mounted in silver-gilt. About 1580. H. 10¼ in. Acquired with the aid of the National Art Collections Fund.   1561–1904

22. WINE-JUG. Chinese porcelain (Wan-Li period) mounted in silver-gilt. Maker's mark, a trefoil in a shaped shield. London hall-mark for 1585–86. H. 10 in. 7914-1862

23. JUG. Siegburg earthenware mounted in silver. Maker's mark, three trefoils slipped in a shaped shield. About 1580. H. 9⅛ in.

130–1908

24. JUG. Rhenish stoneware mounted in silver-gilt. Maker's mark of John Eydes. Exeter mark about 1580. H. 9½ in.

2121–1855

25. COCONUT CUP with silver mounts. About 1580. H. 8½ in. M.357–1927

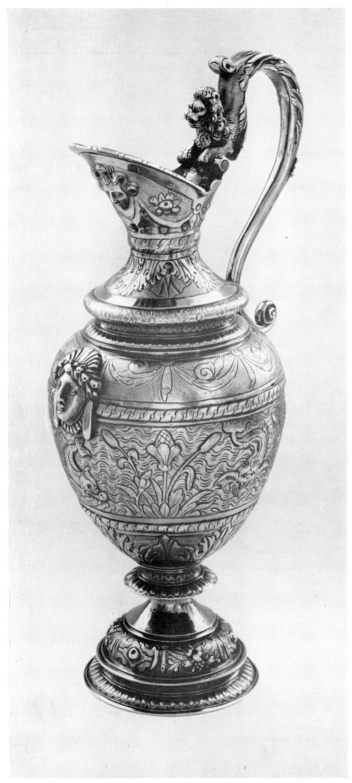

26. EWER. Maker's mark, R S. London hall-mark for 1583–84. H. 13¼ in.   M.250–1924

27. THE MOSTYN SALT. Maker's mark, T in a pearled border. London hall-mark for 1586–87.
H. 16⅛ in.   146–1886

28. DETAIL of the Mostyn Salt. 146–1886

29. COVERED CUP. Maker's mark, three slipped trefoils in a shaped shield. London hall-mark for 1590–91. H. 7½ in. M.356–1927

30. THE VYVYAN SALT. Silver-gilt set with panels of painted glass. Maker's mark, WH with a flower (?). London hall-mark for 1592-93. H. 15¾ in. Acquired with the help of a body of subscribers.

M.273-1925

31. BELL SALT. Maker's mark, NR linked with four pellets. London hall-mark for 1594–95.
H. 9⅛ in.   283–1893

32. THE SMELT CUP. Maker's mark, BL with a woolsack (?). London hall-mark for 1599–1600.
H. 8 in. Given by Miss E. G. Tanner.   M.192–1926

33a. CASKET. Mother-of-pearl mounted in silver-gilt. About 1600. H. 3⅜ in.   M.245–1924

33b. Lid of M.245–1924.

34. WINE-CUP. Gilt. Maker's mark, CG monogram. London hall-mark for 1603–4. H. 5 in.

M.247–1924

35. TANKARD. Gilt. Maker's mark, R M. London hall-mark for 1607-8. H. 8⅓ in.   M.1-1923

36. BASIN. Gilt. Maker's mark, R S. London hall-mark for 1607–8. Diam. 22½ in.   M.6–1961

37. STANDING CUP AND COVER. Gilt. Maker's mark, TYL in monogram. London hall-mark
for 1611–12. H. 18⅝ in.

5964–1859

38a. DETAIL of No. 37.

38b. DETAIL of No. 37.

39. WINE-CUP. Gilt. Maker's mark. E.W. London hall-mark for 1609–10. H. 6⅛ in.   M.246–1924

40. WINE-CUP. Gilt. Maker's mark, CB in monogram. London hall-mark for 1616–17. Acquired under the Bryan Bequest. H. 8½ in. M.20–1934

41. STANDING CUP AND COVER. Coconut mounted in silver. English; about 1610. H. 15½ in.
168–1865

42. STANDING SALT. Gilt. Maker's mark, R.B. London hall-mark for 1614–15. Bequeathed by Mrs. E. K. Hornsby-Drake. H. 16⅜ in.   M.10–1931

43. THE DYNELEY CASKET. Alabaster mounted in silver-gilt. Maker's mark, a trefoil slipped. About 1620. H. 7¾ in. 24–1865

44. TANKARD. Serpentine mounted in silver. Maker's mark, a slipped trefoil in a shaped shield. About 1620. Acquired under the Bryan Bequest. H. 8⅛ in.   M.52–1912

45. THE RICHARD CHESTER CUP. Gilt. Maker's mark, FT in monogram. London hall-mark for 1625–26. H. 17⅛ in.   M.244–1924

46. STANDING-CUP AND COVER. Maker's mark, F. London hall-mark for 1627–28. Given by the Venerable D. Tait, Archdeacon of Rochester. H. 23 in.   M.80–1921

47. WINE-CUP. Maker's mark, RS with an anchor. London hall-mark for 1623–24. Given by Mr. Tufnell Burchell. H. 9¾ in.   142–1901

48. TANKARD. Serpentine mounted in silver-gilt. Maker's mark, WR with an arch. About 1630.
Given by Sir Charles J. Jackson, F.S.A. H. 8⅜ in.   M.92-1914

49. WINE-CUP. Maker's mark, WC with a heart. London hall-mark for 1637–38. H. 6⅝ in.
287–1893

50. BEAKER. About 1640. Given by Sir Paul Makins, Bart. H. 8⅜ in.　　　M.115–1926

51a. WINE-TASTER. Maker's mark, F I above a catherine wheel(?). London hall-mark for 1642–43. Given by Mrs. Adela Temple Willis. Diam. 3⅝ in.　　　　M.14–1935

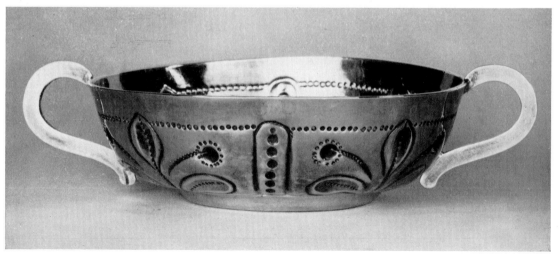

51b. Side view of above.

52. TANKARD WITH SPOUT. Mark of Timothy Skottowe. Norwich hall-mark for 1642–43.
Given by Mr. L. C. Price. H. 4½ in.   M.84–1920

53. FRUIT BOWL. Maker's mark, E.S. London hall-mark for 1649–50. Timmis Bequest. Diam.
10¼ in.   M.83–1933

54. FLAGON. Maker's mark, a hound sejant. London hall-mark for 1646–47. Given by the National Art Collections Fund. H. 10 in.   M.537–1956

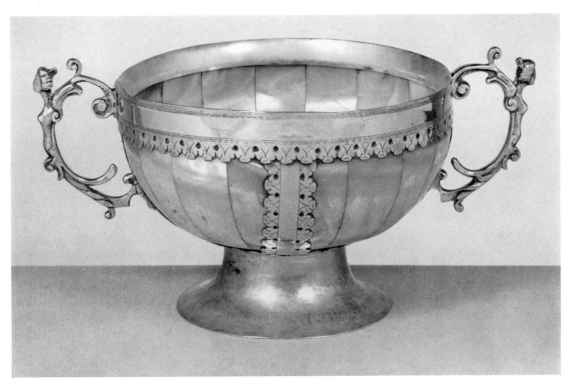

55. CUP. Mother-o'-pearl mounted in silver. About 1650. Alfred Williams Hearn Gift. H. 4 in.
M.46–1923

56. CUP. Maker's mark, SA in monogram. London hall-mark for 1656–57. Acquired under the
Bryan Bequest. H. 3½ in. M.376–1924

57. TANKARD. Maker's mark of John Plummer. York hall-mark for 1657–58. Given by the
National Art Collections Fund. H. 7¼ in.   M.217–1938

58. LID OF TANKARD No. 57 (Arms and crest of Sayer). M.217–1938

59. CUP AND COVER. Maker's mark, SA in a monogram with a mullet. London hall-mark for
1658–59. H. 5⅝ in.   52–1865

60. CUP AND COVER. Gilt. Maker's mark, G.S. with a crook. London hall-mark for 1660–61.
H. 6 in.   7242–1861

61a. MACE OF THE CONSERVATORS OF THE FENS. Gilt. Given by the Honourable Bedford Level Corporation to whom it was presented in 1663. L. 3 ft. 9 in. M.57–1921

61b. Detail.

62. CLOCK. By David Bouquet (d. 1665). H. 7 in.   M.1139–1926

63. THE MOODY SALT. The scroll arms were intended to support a dish. Maker's mark, WH with a cherub. London hall-mark for 1664–65. Frances Reubell Bryan Bequest. H. $7\frac{1}{2}$ in.

M.347–1912

64. SALVER. Maker's mark, DR with two stars. London hall-mark for 1664–65. Diam. 14½ in.

549–1874

65. CUP AND COVER. Gilt with silver casing. Maker's mark, CG monogram with sun. London
hall-mark for 1669–70. H. 7 in.   290–1854

66. TEA-POT. Maker's mark, T.L. London hall-mark for 1670–71. H. 13½ in.

67. TANKARD. Maker's mark of William Ramsey. Newcastle hall-mark about 1670. Given by the
National Art Collections Fund. H. 7 in.   M.180–1938

68. THE STERNE CUP. Gilt. Maker's mark, AC monogram. London hall-mark for 1673–74.
H. 7¾ in.   M.103–1925

69. CUP. Gilt. Maker's mark, IN above a bird. London hall-mark for 1675–76. Bequeathed by
Mrs. Arthur James. H. 4⅛ in.   M.32–1948

70. FLASK. Gilt. Maker's mark, crowned AM monogram. London hall-mark for 1675–76. Given by Mr. Harvey Hadden. H. 13½ in.   M.46a–1914

71. VASE. Gilt. Maker's mark, W.W. with fleur-de-lis. London hall-mark for 1675–76. Given by Mr. Harvey Hadden. H. 14⅛ in.
                                                                    M.46–1914

72. WINE-COOLER. Maker's mark, T I between two quatrefoils. London hall-mark for 1677–78. W. 22½ in.   M.37–1957

73. BEAKER. Maker's mark, T C crowned. London hall-mark for 1680–81. Given by Major A. J. Carter, D.S.O. and his wife. H. 3⅞ in.

M.416-1927

The Guift of Richard Sterne Eqʳ
to yᵉ Honorable East-India-Compᵃ

74. COFFEE-POT. Maker's mark, G.G. London hall-mark for 1681–82. H. 9¾ in.　　02640

75. SUGAR-BOX. Maker's mark, I S monogram. London hall-mark for 1683–84. L. 8½ in.   53–1865

76. INK-STAND. Maker's mark of Anthony Nelme. Late 17th century. W. 7½ in.   M.579–1924

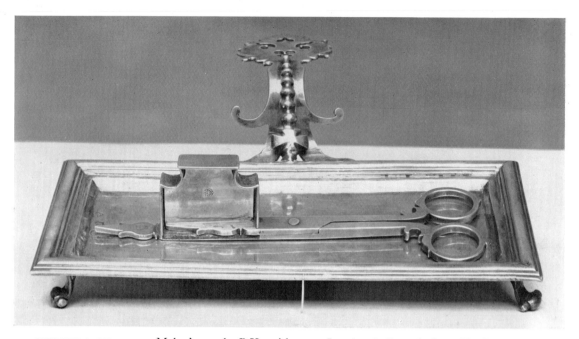

77. SNUFFERS AND PAN. Maker's mark, P.K. with star. London hall-mark for 1682–83.
L. (pan) 9 in.   115, 115a–1864

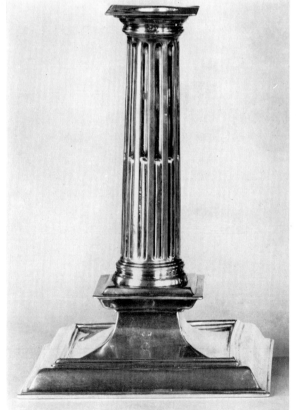

78. CANDLESTICK. Maker's mark, RM monogram. London hall-mark for 1682–83. H. 7 in.
M.562–1911

79. CUP AND COVER. Maker's mark, IB with a stag. London hall-mark for 1683–84. Given by Col. Sir C. Wyndham Murray, K.C.B. H. $7\frac{1}{8}$ in.   M.129–1922

80. CUP. Maker's mark, IR monogram. London hall-mark for 1683–84. Bequeathed by the Reverend T. W. Webb. H. $3\frac{7}{8}$ in.   238–1885

81a. THE CALVERLEY TOILET SERVICE. Maker's mark, W.t. with a knot. London hall-mark for 1683–84. Bequeathed by Sir Walter Calverley Trevelyan, Bart.   240–240m–1879

81b. DETAIL OF CASKET, Calverley Toilet Service.

82a. LID OF CASKET, Calverley Toilet Service (see no. 81a). W. 9⅝ in.

82b. DETAIL OF MIRROR, Calverley Toilet Service.

83. SALVER, Calverley Toilet Service. Diam. $11\frac{1}{2}$ in.

84. OIL PAINTING in the style of Edwaert Collyer (fl. 1662–96) showing a tankard with the London hall-mark for 1688–89 and a salt-cellar of about the same date. Given by Mr. L. A. Crichton through the National Art Collections Fund. P.28–1923

85. OIL PAINTING by Pieter Roestraten (1627–1700) showing a cup with provincial hall-marks about 1660 (also a German cup and cover, about 1650). Bequeathed by L. A. Crichton.   P.3–1939

86. OIL PAINTING by Pieter Roestraten (1627–1700). Showing a cup and cover about 1660 (also a nautilus shell cup mounted in silver-gilt, German, about 1620). Bequeathed by L. A. Crichton.   P.4–1939

87. TANKARD. Maker's mark, IS above a cinquefoil. London hall-mark for 1684–85. From the Arthur James Collection, bequeathed by his wife. H. 8½ in.　　　　　　M.31–1948

88a. PORRINGER. Maker's mark, RP. London hall-mark for 1684–85. Frank Smith Bequest.
W. 6⅞ in.   M.420–1922

88b. SNUFF BOX with a view of Norwich(?). About 1685. Maker's mark, IH between two stars.
Ethel Gurney Bequest. W. 3¾ in.   M.153–1939

89. TEA-POT. Gilt. Maker's mark, R.H. About 1685. H. 5¾ in.   M.48–1939

90a. BOX (lid). Maker's mark, PD crowned. About 1685. Croft Lyons Bequest. W. 3⅞ in.

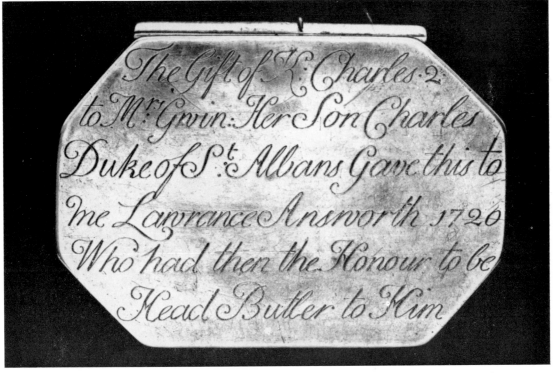

90b. Bottom view.   M.700–1926

91. BEAKER. Gilt, forming part of a pocket canteen. Maker's mark, TT crowned. About 1690.
H. 3¼ in.   M.62-1949

92. FOLDING KNIFE, FORK and SPOON. Gilt, forming part of the canteen shown in 91. The
spoon L. 7 in.   M.62a to c–1949

93. CASTER. Maker's mark, LB crowned. London hall-mark for 1692–93. Given by Mr. and Mrs. W. W. Simpson through the National Art Collections Fund. H. 6⅛ in.   M.147–1913

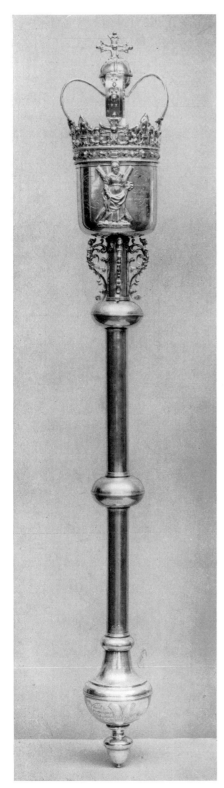

94a. MACE OF THE COURT LEET OF ST. ANDREWS, HOLBORN. Parcel-gilt. Maker's mark of Benjamin Pyne. London hall-mark for 1694–95. Given by Mr. William Burchell. L. 42⅝ in.
94b. DETAIL.

808–1897

95. SNUFFERS AND STAND. Maker's mark, TB. Engraved with the arms of Whitney. London hall-mark for 1696–97. Croft Lyons Bequest. H. 4¼ in. (without snuffers).   M.831, 831a–1926

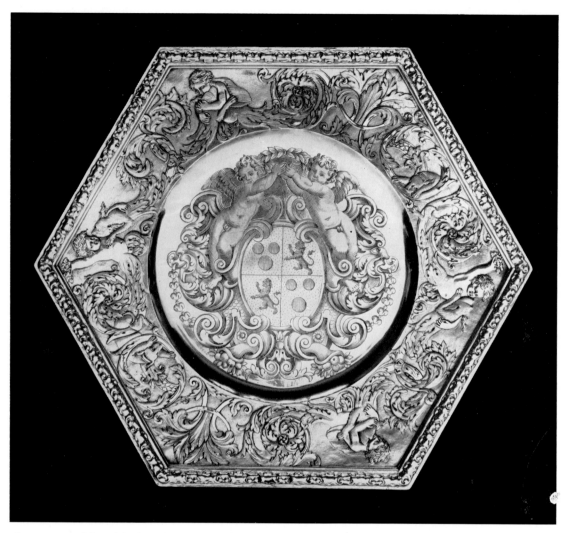

96. WAITER. Gilt, with chased ornament after Jean le Pautre (1618–82); engraved with the arms of Sir William Courtenay of Powderham Castle, Devon. Maker's mark of Benjamin Pyne. London hall-mark for 1698–99. Acquired under the Bryan Bequest. W. 9½ in.   M.77–1947

97. EWER. Gilt. Maker's mark of David Willaume. London hall-mark for 1700–1. H. 8⅛ in.
Bond Gift.   822–1890

98. DETAIL of No. 97. Arms of Hill, cos. Lancs. and Salop.

99. TANKARD. Maker's mark of John Downes. London hall-mark for 1701–2. Bequeathed by the Reverend John Evelyn Stacye. H. 6⅞ in.   907–1905

100. BRACKET CLOCK. Ebony case with silver mounts engraved with the arms, crest and cypher of Charles Bodville Robartes, 2nd Earl of Radnor (1685–1723). Movement signed 'Charles Gretton in Fleet Street'. About 1700. Given by Mr. Herbert Sleigh. H. 14 in.   M.54–1943

101. TAPERSTICK. Maker's mark, BA with two rosettes. London hall-mark for 1702–3. H. 5⅜ in.
M.838–1928

102. TAPERSTICK. London hall-mark for 1702–3. Inscribed 'Queen Anne 1702', and 'His Highness Prince George LSS Anno Dom; 1702'. Maker's mark of Edmund Procter. Purchased under the Bryant Bequest. H. 4½ in.   M.235–1924

103. WALL-SCONCE. Maker's mark of John Rand. London hall-mark for 1703–4. H. 8¼ in.
816–1890

104. CHOCOLATE-POT. Maker's mark of William Fawdery. London hall-mark for 1704–5.
T. H. Cobb Bequest. H. 10 in.   M.1819–1944

105. CUP. Maker's mark of John Sutton. London hall-mark for 1705–6. H. 4½ in.   3635–1856

106. TEA-POT WITH STAND AND LAMP. Maker's mark of Simon Pantin. London hall-mark for
1705–6. Harvey Haddon Gift. H. 5⅞ in.   M.172 to 172b–1919

107. FLASK. Engraved with the arms of General Charles Churchill (d. 1714). Maker's mark of
Pierre Platel. H. 15⅞ in.   M.854–1927

108. SCONCE. Engraved with the arms of William Herbert, 2nd Marquess of Powis. Maker's mark of John Boddington. London hall-mark for 1710–11. H. 13½ in.   M.50–1959

109. SALVER. Gilt. London hall-mark for 1717–18. Maker's mark of William Lukin. Engraved with the arms of Richard Ingram, 5th Viscount Ingram impaling those of his wife Lady Anne Howard, surrounded by figures of the Four Elements and signed by Joseph Sympson. Diam. 14½ in.

M.41–1947

110. 'A tea-party in the time of George I.' Oil painting. Given by the National Art Collections Fund.   P.9–1934

III. CASTER. Maker's mark of Simon Pantin. London hall-mark for 1716–17. Harvey Haddon Gift. H. 8⅜ in. M.178–1919

112. CASTER. Maker's mark of Thomas Fowler. London hall-mark for 1708–9. Harvey Haddon Gift. H. 9⅛ in. M.181–1919

113. TEA-POT. Maker's marks of Jonathan Lambe and Thomas Tearle. London hall-mark for 1718–19. Given by Mr. and Mrs. W. W. Simpson through the National Art Collections Fund. H. 6⅝ in.   M.166–1914

114. TEA-POT. Maker's mark of James Smith. London hall-mark for 1719-20. Given by Miss Eleanor Trouncer. H. 4 in.   M.228-1939

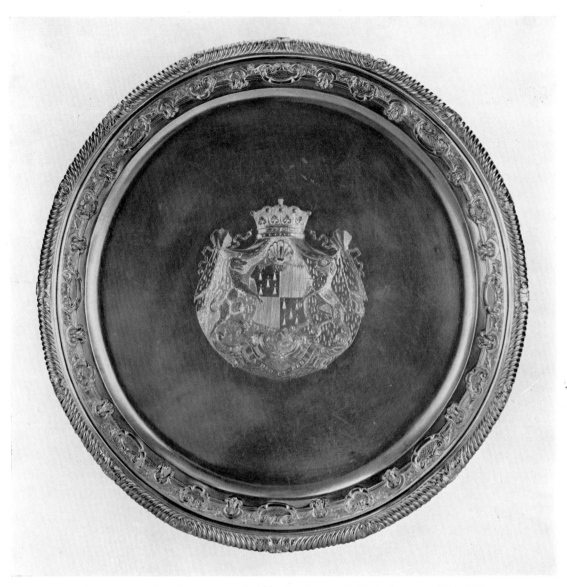

115. SALVER. Gilt. Engraved with the arms of Philip Stanhope, 4th Earl of Chesterfield. Maker's mark of John Hugh Le Sage. London hall-mark for 1727–28. Diam. 14¾ in.   M.72–1950

116. TEA-KETTLE STAND. No marks. About 1725. H. 27½ in.   M.37–1956

117. TEA-KETTLE AND STAND. Maker's mark of Charles Kandler. London, 1727–37. H. 13¼ in.
M.49–1939

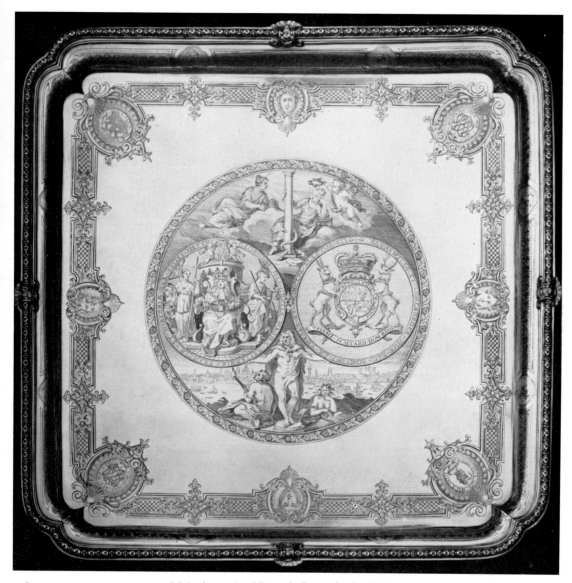

118. THE WALPOLE SALVER. Maker's mark of Paul de Lamerie. Probably engraved by William Hogarth. London hall-mark for 1728–29. Purchased with the aid of contributions from the Worshipful Company of Goldsmiths, the National Art Collections Fund and the Pilgrim Trust. W. 19½ in.   M.9–1956

119. CHOCOLATE-POT. London hall-mark for 1722–23. Given by Major A. J. Carter, D.S.O. and his wife. H. 9¼ in

M.379–1927

120. CUP. Maker's mark of John Eckfourd. London hall-mark for 1722–23. Given by Major
A. J. Carter, D.S.O., and his wife. H. 10¼ in.   M.399–1927

121. CANDLESTICK. Maker's mark of David Tanqueray. London hall-mark for 1720–21.
Timmis Bequest. H. 7 in.   M.66–1933

122. CANDLESTICK. Maker's mark of David Green. London hall-mark for 1720–21. Harvey
Haddon Gift. H. 6⅝ in.   M.174–1919

123a. INKSTAND. Engraved with the Arms and Crest of Vernon, Co. Chester. Maker's mark of Paul de Lamerie. London hall-mark for 1729–30. Gurney Bequest. W. 8¾ in. M.155-1939

123b. SUGAR BOWL. Engraved with the Arms of Baron, Co. Essex, or Hill, Co. Som., impaling another. Maker's mark of Edward Cornock. London hall-mark for 1730–31. Gurney Bequest. H. 3¼ in. M.164-1939

124. TEA-KETTLE AND STAND. Engraved with a coat of arms, impaling Lambert. Maker's mark of Simon Pantin. London hall-mark for 1730–31. Timmis Bequest. H. 14⅛ in.   M.73-1933

125. SALVER. Gilt Maker's mark of Thomas Farren. London hall-mark for 1733–34. Given by Mrs. Anne C. Comyns in memory of her husband, Charles Harling Comyns. W. $14\frac{7}{8}$ in.   M.3–1926

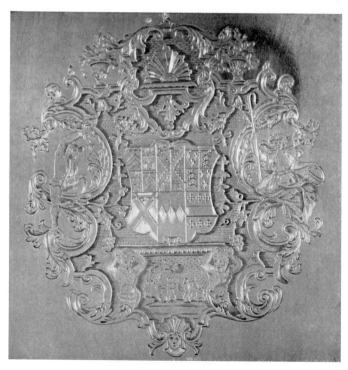

126. DETAIL of Pl. 125. Arms of John Sharles Barrington, of Waltham Cross, Essex. d. 1788. Showing his descent from George, Duke of Clarence, and Isabella Neville, daughter of the Kingmaker.

127. CASTER. Maker's mark of Paul de Lamerie. London hall-mark for 1734–35. Gurney Bequest. H. 6¼ in.   M.157–1939

128. TEA-CADDY. Engraved with the Arms of Knipe with another in pretence. Maker's mark of Paul de Lamerie. London hall-mark for 1735–36. Gurney Bequest. H. 5½ in.   M.156–1939

129. EWER. Silver-gilt. Made by Paul de Lamerie. With arms of Philip Yorke, Baron Hardwicke, 1736 (transposed hall-mark). H. 19½ in.   M.16–1954

130. COVERED CUP. Maker's mark of Edward Vincent. London hall-mark for 1736–37. Bond Gift. H. 12¼ in.   819–1890

131. SPOON TRAY. Engraved with the arms of Eyre quartering others. Maker's mark indecipherable. London hall-mark for 1736–37. Given by Mr. Douglas Eyre. L. 6¾ in.   M.41–1922

132. ARM-BADGE. Worn by one of the crew of the Admiralty barge. Maker's mark of William Lukin. London hall-mark for 1736–37. Given by the Lords Commissioners of the Admiralty. H. 10 in.   8879–1863

133. THE NEWDEGATE CENTREPIECE. Maker's mark of Paul de Lamerie. London hall-mark for 1743–44. Purchased with the aid of a number of donations. H. 9⅞ in. 48189   M. 149–1919

134. DETAIL of No. 133 showing the top of the central dish. Engraved with the arms of Sir Roger Newdegate impaling those of his wife, Sophia Conyers.

135. TEA-POT. Maker's mark of John Wirgman. London hall-mark for 1748–49. Arthur Hurst Bequest. H. 4⅝ in.   M.60–1940

136. CHAMBER CANDLESTICK. Gilt. Maker's mark of Paul de Lamerie. London hall-mark for 1748–49. Arthur Hurst Bequest.   M.77–1940

137. CREAM JUG. Gilt. No marks. About 1750. H. 5⅛ in.   M.248–1921

138. CAKE-BASKET (end view). Maker's mark of S. Herbert & Co. London hall-mark for 1753–54. Given by Mr. Eric M. Browett, in memory of his wife, Ada Mary Browett. W. 14½ in. M.154–1937

139. TEA-CADDY. Maker's mark of William Shaw and William Preist. London hall-mark for
1759–60. W. T. Johnson Bequest.   M.1772–1944

140. TEA-CADDY WITH SPOON. Maker's mark of Edward Wakelin. London hall-mark for 1762–63. W. T. Johnson Bequest. H. 9¼ in.   M.1675–1944

141. DESIGN for a soup tureen with the arms of Thomas Coke, Earl of Leicester. Signed by Nicholas Sprimont. Given by Mr. A. G. B. Russell through the National Art Collections Fund.

E.2606–1917

142. CHEESE PLATE. Engraved with the arms of Brownlow Cecil, 9th Earl of Exeter. Maker's mark of Edward Wakelin. London hall-mark for 1760. H. 5⅞ in.   M.32–1961

143. TRADE CARD of Thomas Heming showing, in the top left-hand corner, a representation of the cup illustrated as plate 144. About 1765.

144. CUP. Silver-Gilt. Maker's mark of Thomas Heming. London hall-mark for 1759–60.
Given by the Esso Petroleum Company Limited. H. 15½ in.   M.41–1959

145. COFFEE-POT. Maker's mark of David Smith and Robert Sharp. London hall-mark for 1765–66. Arthur Hurst Bequest. H. 10½ in. M.48–1940

146. COFFEE-POT. Maker's mark of William Tuite. London hall-mark for 1762–63. Bond Gift.
H. 18½ in.   494–1875

147. TEA-CADDY. Mark of Pierre Gillois. London hall-mark for 1766–67. Given by Mrs. Elton
B. Ede. H. 5¾ in.   M.299–1923

148. TEA-URN. Maker's mark of Thomas Whipham and Charles Wright. London hall-mark for 1767–68. (The cover is a restoration.) Given by Mr. C. D. Rotch. H. 21 in.　　M.4–1918

149. COVERED CUP. Gilt. Maker's mark of Walton Brind. London hall-mark for 1769–70.
H. 17⅛ in.   46–1864

150. COVERED CUP. Maker's mark of Louisa Courtauld and George Cowles. London hall-mark for 1771–72. Bond Gift. H. 14⅝ in.   804–1890

151. CAKE-BASKET. Maker's mark of Richard Mills. London. hall-mark for 1771–72. W. T. Johnson Bequest. W. 13⅞ in.   M.1696–1944

152. SUGAR-BASIN WITH BLUE GLASS LINER. Maker's mark, C. H. London hall-mark for 1772–73. Frank Smith Bequest. H. 3⅝ in.   M.440–1922

153. VASE. Gilt. Maker's mark of John Arnell. London hall-mark for 1772–73. H. 8⅓ in.   55–1865

154. TEA-CADDY. Maker's mark of Louisa Courtauld and George Cowles. London hall-mark for 1773–74. Engraved with a crest and with the Chinese characters for 'upper', 'spring' and 'direction'. Given by Mrs. Penryn Milsted. H. 3½ in.   M.28–1934

155. COVERED CUP. Maker's mark of William Cripps. London hall-mark for 1774–75. H. 16⅝ in.

493–1875

156. CANDLESTICK. Maker's mark of G. Ashforth & Co. Sheffield hall-mark for 1774–75.
Bond Gift. H. 11½ in.   832–1890

157. CANDLESTICK. Maker's mark, IC. Sheffield hall-mark for 1776–77. R. J. Dyson Bequest.
H. 12¼ in.   M.23–1943

158. WINE-COOLER. Maker's mark of Fred Kandler. London hall-mark for 1775–76. Given in memory of Alexander Allan Paton, C.B., by his sister Mary Paton. H. 7½ in.   M.596–1936

159. EPERGNE. Maker's mark of Thomas Powell. London hall-mark for 1778–79. Given. H. 14½ in.

M.19–1958

160. SAUCE-TUREEN. Maker's mark of Matthew Boulton & J. Fothergill. Birmingham hall-mark for 1776–77. Given by Mr. M. L. Horn. W. 10 in.   M.432–1936

161. HOT-WATER JUG. Maker's mark of John Carter. London hall-mark for 1775–76. W. T. Johnson Bequest. H. 12 in.   M.1680–1944

162. COFFEE-POT. Maker's mark of Charles Woodward. London hall-mark for 1776–77.
H. 13½ in.   752–1877

163. CHOCOLATE-POT. Maker's mark of Henry Greenway. London hall-mark for 1777–78.
H. 12¾ in.   460–1875

164. TEA-CADDY. Maker's mark of Thomas Heming. London hall-mark for 1778–79. H. 9⅛ in.

503–1875

165. SUGAR-BASKET WITH BLUE GLASS LINER. Maker's mark of John Swift. London hall-mark for 1778–79. Henry L. Florence Bequest. H. 4⅓ in.   M.216–1917

166. VASE AND COVER. A coconut mounted in silver-gilt and set with Wedgwood blue jasper-ware cameos of the Three Graces and of Omphale. No marks. H. 7⅝ in. 815–1891

167. CREAM-JUG. Maker's mark of Andrew Fogelberg & Stephen Gilbert. London hall-mark for 1780–81. Set with medallions by W. Brown after Tassie's copies of gems. W. T. Johnson Bequest. H. 5⅜ in.   M.1759–1944

168. CREAM-JUG. Gilt. Maker's mark of Robert Hennell. London hall-mark for 1785–86. H. 7⅛ in.

757–1877

169. TEA-CADDY. Maker's mark of J. Hampston & J. Prince. York hall-mark for 1784–85. Arthur Hurst Bequest. H. 4½ in.   M.21–1940

170. TEA-POT. Maker's mark of J. Hampston & J. Prince. York hall-mark for 1784–85. Arthur Hurst Bequest. H. 5 in.   M.63–1940

171. TEA-POT. Maker's mark of Andrew Fogelberg & Stephen Gilbert. London hall-mark for 1784–85. Given by Mr. C. D. Rotch through the National Art Collections Fund.   M.47–1960

172. CRUET FRAME. Maker's mark of John Schofield. London hall-mark for 1789–90. Given by Mr. C. D. Rotch through the National Art Collections Fund.   M.46 to h–1960

173. VASE (tea-caddy?). One of a set of three. Maker's mark of Robert Sharp. London hall-mark for 1785–86. Bequeathed by Miss M. B. Hudson. H. 8⅝ in.   M.394–1922

174. TAPERSTICK. Maker's mark of J. Parsons & Co. Sheffield hall-mark for 1787–88.   387–1871

175. CRUET-FRAME WITH CUT-GLASS CRUETS. Maker's mark of Hester Bateman. London hall-mark for 1788–89. Bequeathed by Miss Laura Metford Badcock and Miss Mary Metford Badcock. H. 9 in.   M.103–1933

176. SAUCE-TUREEN. Maker's mark of Henry Cowper. London hall-mark for 1788–89. W. 7½ in.
578–1874

177. TEA-POT WITH STAND. Maker's mark of Henry Chawner. London hall-mark for 1791–92.
Given by Miss Maria Willis. Tea-pot H. 6 in.; stand L. 6⅝ in. 1317 & a–1900

178. CREAM-JUG. Maker's mark of Chas. Hougham(?). London hall-mark for 1790–91. Arthur Hurst Bequest. H. 6¾ in.   M.129-1940

179. HOT-WATER JUG. Maker's mark of Peter and Anne Bateman. London hall-mark for
1793-94. Bequeathed by Miss M. B. Hudson. H. 13⅛ in.   M.395-1922

180. DESIGN by J. Boileau for the Doncaster Race Cup for 1800.   8529B

181. CUP & COVER. Gilt. Maker's mark of John Schofield. London hall-mark for 1795–96.
Lady Henriques Bequest. H. 14 in.   M.78–1953

182. TEA-POT. Maker's mark of Jonathan Alleine. London hall-mark for 1798–99. Given in memory of Allan Paton, C.B., by his sister Mary Paton. H. 4½ in. M.598–1936

183. TEA-POT. Maker's mark of Peter, Ann and William Bateman. London hall-mark for 1802–3. Henry L. Florence Bequest. H. 7⅓ in. M.217–1917

184. SAUCE-TUREEN. Maker's mark of R. & S. Hennell. London hall-mark for 1805–6. R. J. Dyson Bequest. H. 6¼ in.   M.47–1943

185a. SALT-CELLAR. Maker's mark of Daniel Pontifex(?). London hall-mark for 1802–3.
Arthur Hurst Bequest. H. 2⅛ in.   M.96–1940

185b. SALT-CELLAR. Maker's mark of William Abdy. London hall-mark for 1803–4. R. J.
Dyson Bequest. H. 3¼ in.   M.41–1943

186. THE TRAFALGAR VASE. Maker's mark of Digby Scott and Benjamin Smith. London hall-mark for 1805-6. Designed by John Flaxman, R.A. One of a series of vases made to the order of Lloyd's Patriotic Fund for presentation to admirals and captains at the Battle of Trafalgar. Bond Gift. H. 17 in.

803-1890

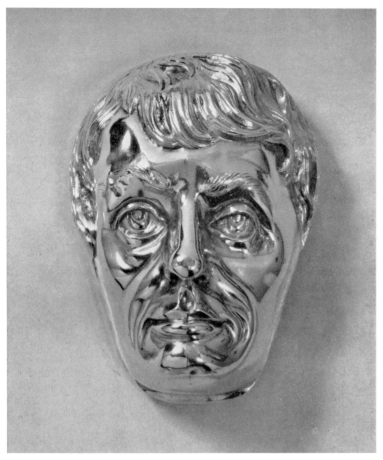

187. SNUFF-BOX. Gilt; in the form of a mask of Lord Nelson. The cover of oak from H.M.S. *Bellerophon*, inscribed 'Calvi, Copenhagen, Trafalgar, Oct. 21, 1805'. Bond Gift. H. 3½ in.

835–1890

188a. LAMP. Gilt. Maker's mark of Digby Scott and Benjamin Smith. London hall-mark for
1806–7. W. T. Johnson Bequest. H. 2¼ in. M.1700–1944

188b. SUGAR-VASE. Gilt. Maker's mark of Digby Scott and Benjamin Smith. London hall-mark
for 1805–6. Made to the order of Rundell, Bridge and Rundell. Engraved with the crest of
Archbishop Manners Sutton. Given in memory of Allan Paton, C.B., by his sister, Mary Paton.
H. 6¾ in. M.597–1936

189. SAUCE-TUREEN. Parcel-gilt. Maker's mark of John Edward. London hall-mark for 1806–7. Part of the service presented to Sir Arthur Wellesley, K.B., by the officers of the army of the Deccan, 1803. H. 8 in.   W.M.750–1948

190. CANDELABRUM. Parcel-gilt. Maker's mark of Joseph Preedy. London hall-mark for 1806–7.
Presented to Sir Arthur Wellesley, K.B., by the officers of the army of the Deccan, 1803. H. 31 in.
W.M.764–1948

191. DESIGN FOR A CANDELABRUM with the arms of George Hamilton-Gordon, 4th Earl of Aberdeen (succeeded 1802 died 1819). By Charles Catton, junior (1756–1819). About 1804.   112

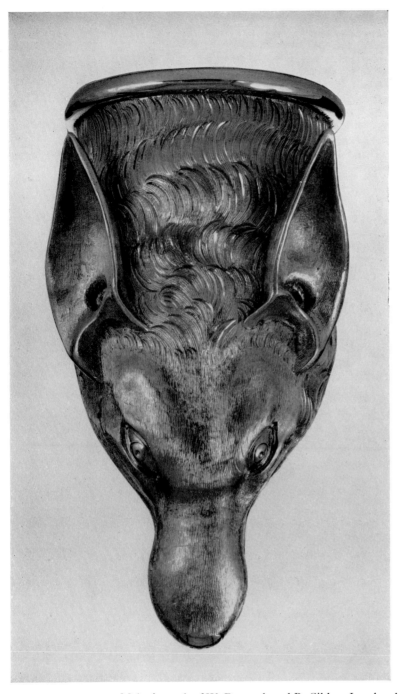

192. STIRRUP-CUP. Maker's mark of W. Burwash and R. Sibley. London hall-mark for 1807–8.
Croft Lyons Bequest. H. 5¾ in. M.867–1926

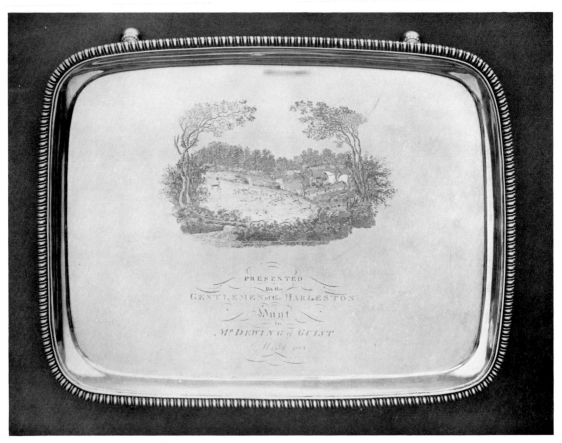

193. SALVER. Maker's mark of Ann Robertson. Newcastle hall-mark for 1808–9. Engraved with a hunting-scene by Thomas Bewick (1753–1828). Given by Mr. Kerrison Preston through the National Art Collections Fund. W. 12⅝ in.   M.10–1943

194. CRUET-FRAME fitted with a mustard pot and six cut-glass bottles. Maker's mark, CC. London hall-mark for 1810–11. Bequeathed in fulfilment of the wishes of John Irving. H. 9⅞ in.

M.354–1921

195. SUGAR-VASE. Gilt. Maker's mark of Benjamin and James Smith. London hall-mark for 1810–11. Part of the Duke of Wellington's ambassador's service, 1814. H. 8 in.   W.M.361–1948

196. CENTRE-PIECE. Parcel-gilt. Maker's mark of Paul Storr. London hall-mark for 1810–11. Presented to Sir Arthur Wellesley by the field officers of the Army of Portugal in commemoration of the battles of Roliça and Vimiera, in 1808. H. 33 in.   W.M.799–1948

197. CENTRE-PIECE. Parcel gilt. Maker's mark of Paul Storr. London hall-mark for 1811-12.
Made to the order of Rundell, Bridge and Rundell for presentation by the General Officers
originally landed at Figueras in Portugal, 1808. H. 21¾ in.   W.M.798-1948

198. FRUIT STAND. Maker's mark of Paul Storr. London hall-mark for 1812–13. Given by Baroness von Schlippenbach. H. 12⅝ in.   M.49–1960

199a. COASTER. Gilt. Maker's mark of Paul Storr. London hall-mark for 1814–15. Made to the order of Rundell, Bridge and Rundell. Part of the Duke of Wellington's ambassador's service, 1814. H. 5¾ in.   W.M.441–1948

199b. COASTER. Maker's mark indecipherable. Sheffield hall-mark for 1815–16. R. J. Dyson Bequest. H. 2¾ in.   M.26–1943

200. CANDLESTICK. Gilt. Maker's mark of Paul Storr. London hall-mark for 1814–15. Made to the order of Rundell, Bridge and Rundell. Engraved with the cypher of the Duke and Duchess of Cumberland. Given by Mr. Lionel A. Crichton. H. 8¾ in.   M.57–1925

201. CANDELABRUM. Gilt. Maker's mark of Benjamin Smith. London hall-mark for 1816–17. Made to the order of Green, Ward and Green for presentation to the Duke of Wellington from the Merchants and Bankers of the City of London. (Converted so as to burn colza oil, instead of candles, in 1824–25). H. 4 ft. 9 in.   W.M.804–1948

202. VASE. Gilt. Maker's mark, W.E. London hall-mark for 1816–17. Bond Gift. H. 9¾ in.
834–1890

203. SAUCE-TUREEN. Maker's mark of Paul Storr. London hall-mark for 1819–20. H. 7⅜ in.
472–1864

204. TEA-CADDY. Maker's mark, W.E. London hall-mark for 1821–22. R. J. Dyson Bequest.
M.36–1943

205. DESIGN by Thomas Stothard, R.A. (1755–1839) for the Wellington Shield. Diam. 3ft. 4 in.

1202

206. THE WELLINGTON SHIELD. Gilt. Maker's mark of Benjamin Smith. London hall-mark about 1822. Made to the order of Green, Ward and Green for presentation by the Merchants and Bankers of the City of London to the Duke of Wellington. Diam. 3 ft. 4 in.   W.M.806–1948

207. SALVER. Gilt. Maker's mark of Peter Rundell. London hall-mark for 1822–23. The St. George and the Dragon probably designed by Benedetto Pistrucci (1784–1855) the border adapted from the frieze of the Parthenon. Diam. 28 in.   M.67–1950

208. SALVER. Maker's mark of John Angell. London hall-mark for 1823–24. Given by Mr. Lionel van Oven. Diam. 19½ in.   62–1905

209. THE WATERLOO VASE. Gilt. Maker's mark of Benjamin Smith. London hall-mark for 1825–26. Made to the order of Green, Ward and Green for presentation by a body of subscribers to the Duke of Wellington (the plinth made in the same year by Robert Garrard). H. 25¾ in.

W.M.800–1948

210. WEYMOUTH REGATTA CUP. Gilt. Maker's mark of Rebecca Emes and Edward Barnard. London hall-mark for 1827–28. Bond Gift. H. 15½ in.   845–1890

211. TEA-POT. Maker's mark of William Edwards. London hall-mark for 1827–28. R. J. Dyson Bequest. H. 5⅜ in.   M.33–1943